How Do They Grow?

From Kitten to Cat

by Jillian Powell

HODDER
Wayland

an imprint of Hodder Children's Books

© 2001 White-Thomson Publishing Ltd

Produced for Hodder Wayland by
White-Thomson Publishing Ltd
2/3 St. Andrew's Place
Lewes, East Sussex
BN7 1UP

Editor: Sarah Doughty
Designer: Tessa Barwick
Text consultant: Jessica Buss
Language consultant: Norah Granger

Published in Great Britain in 2001 by Hodder Wayland,
an imprint of Hodder Children's Books.

British Cataloguing in Publication Data
   Powell, Jillian
      From Kitten to Cat. – (How do they Grow?)
      1. Kittens – Development – Juvenile literature 2. Cats –
      Physiology – Juvenile literature
      I. Title
      636.8

ISBN 0 7502 3862 3

Printed and bound in Italy by G. Canale & C.S.p.A.

Hodder Children's Books
A division of Hodder Headline Ltd
338 Euston Road, London NW1 3BH

Contents

Words in **bold** in the text can be found in the glossary on page 30.

A cat gives birth

This cat is giving birth to kittens. The first kitten has just been born.

There are four kittens in this **litter**.
They are tiny and wet. The mother is tired.
She sleeps with her kittens.

Newborn kittens

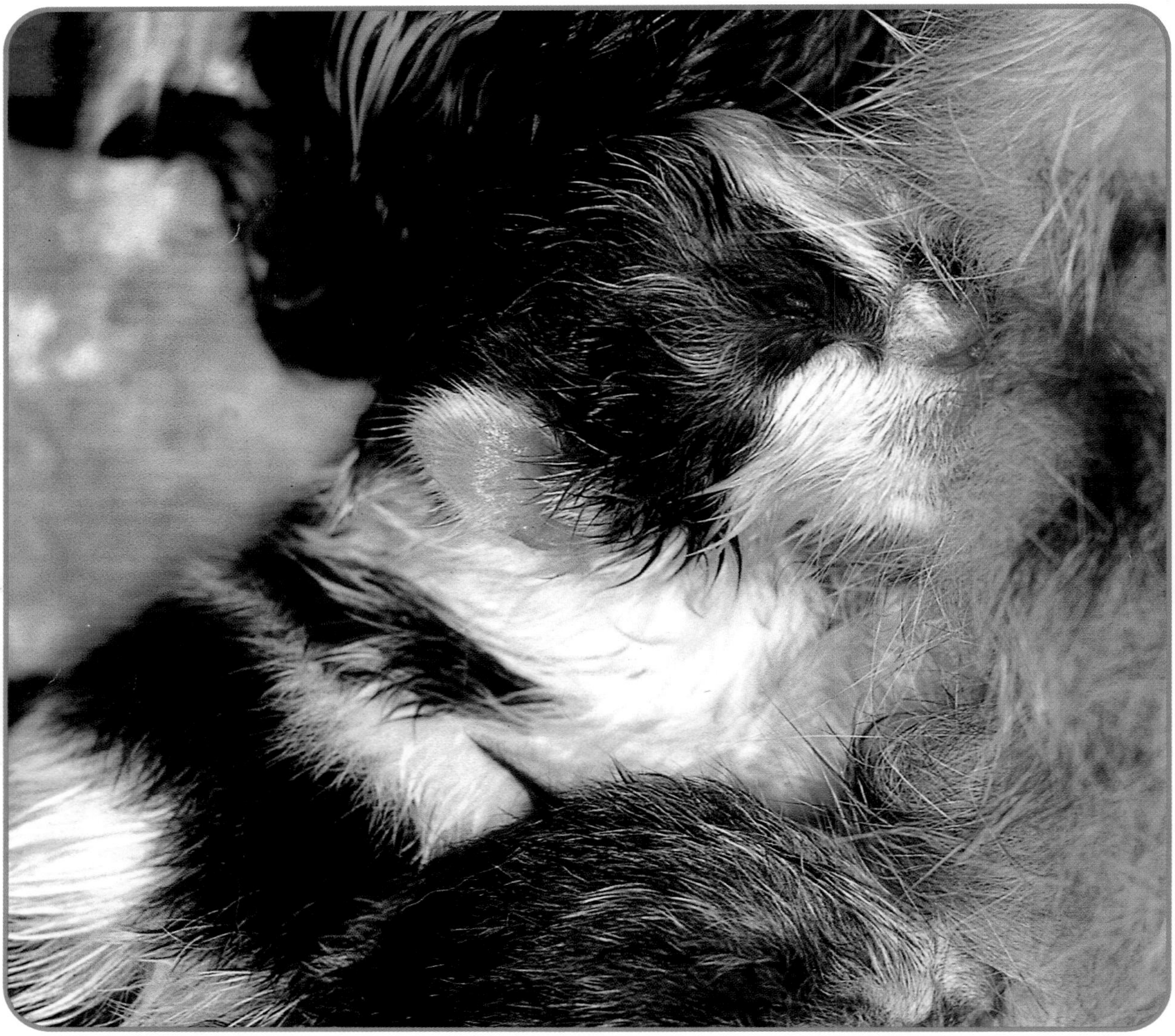

The mother feeds her kittens with her milk.
The milk helps them to grow strong and
fight off **germs**.

The kittens snuggle close to their mother to keep warm. After feeding, some of the kittens fall asleep.

The first few days

For a few days, the kittens just sleep and drink milk. Their mother keeps them clean and warm.

These kittens are a week old. They cannot open their eyes yet. Their legs are floppy and weak. They wriggle around.

Getting bigger

This kitten is two weeks old. Its eyes are now open and it can see. Fur is growing on its ears and nose.

This kitten can now stand up as its legs are growing stronger. Its legs are still wobbly when it tries to walk.

Becoming playful

This kitten is three weeks old. It can walk and run around. Now the kitten wants to play.

The kitten learns to jump and **pounce** and use its paws and claws. It likes to chase and catch toys as if it is **hunting** mice.

Feeding and keeping clean

When they are four weeks old, the kittens grow
their first teeth. They can start
to eat kitten food.

14

This kitten can **groom** itself. It licks its paw to
wash its face. The kitten keeps its fur clean by
licking it all over.

Ready for a new home

This kitten is growing fast. It will soon be ready to leave its mother and go to a new home.

When a kitten is over eight weeks old it is ready to go to a new owner. The kitten needs to be handled gently so it feels safe.

Staying indoors

The kitten must stay indoors until it is
12 weeks old. This keeps it safe from germs.

The vet checks that the kitten is healthy. She gives it **vaccinations** to fight diseases such as cat flu.

Keeping a healthy coat

The kitten feels safe and happy in its new home. It washes itself every day to keep clean.

The new owner grooms the kitten twice a week.
This brushes out the old fur which the kitten
might swallow.

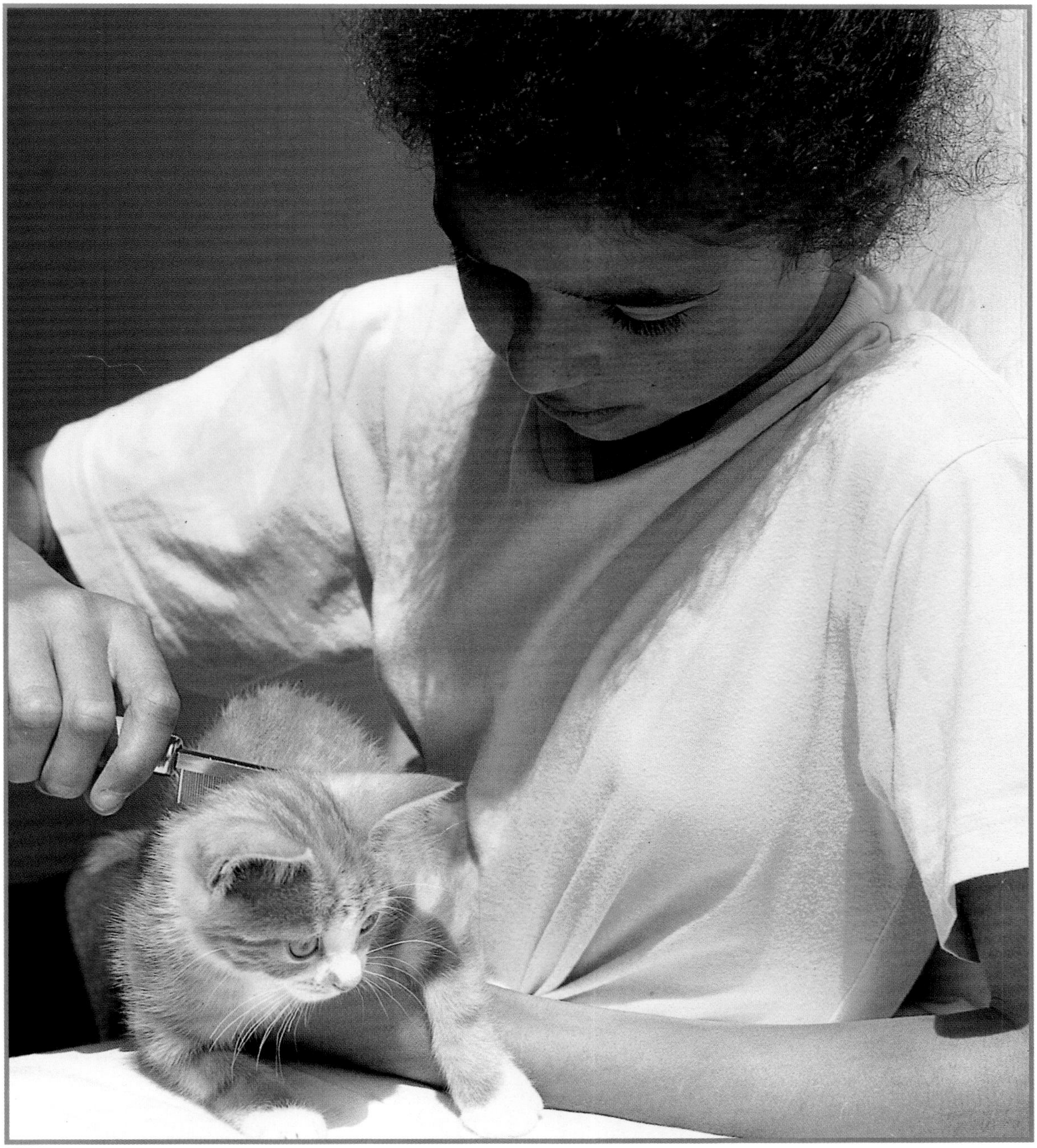

scratching and rubbing

A cat uses its claws to dig, to climb and to hold on. It uses a **scratching post** indoors to sharpen its claws.

22

Outside, a kitten can sharpen its claws on trees. Cats leave a **scent** on trees that tells other cats where they have been.

Eating and playing

A kitten eats three or four small meals every day.
The kitten food helps it to grow bigger
and stronger.

24

The kitten loves to play. It plays with toys which teach it to chase and catch.

Exploring and climbing

The kitten likes to explore. Its long whiskers help it to measure spaces. Its eyes can see well even when it is dark.

26

The kitten has grown into a young cat. Its legs are long and strong and it can jump and climb. Its tail helps it to balance.

Having Kittens

This cat is fully grown. She has **mated** with a **male** cat. Kittens have begun to grow inside her.

28

After the kittens are born, the cat will feed, wash and look after them. Each kitten will grow up to be a strong, healthy cat.

Glossary

Germs Tiny particles around us that can carry diseases.

Groom To keep an animal's fur clean.

Hunting Chasing after another animal for food.

Litter All the young animals born to the same mother at the same time.

Male The opposite sex to female. The male is able to father babies, a female is able to become a mother.

Mated When a male and female have come together to have babies. A male gives a female a seed which makes a female egg grow into a baby animal.

Pounce To jump on something suddenly.

Scent An animal's smell.

Scratching post An object that a cat can use to run its claws up and down.

Vaccinations Injections given with a needle into the skin that protect animals and people from diseases.

Further information

Books

Cats and Kittens (Usborne First Pets series) by Katherine Starke (Usborne, 1998)

Find out about Animals by Steve Pollock (BBC Big Books, 1995)

Kitten (See How They Grow series) by Angela Royston (Dorling Kindersley, 1998)

Kittens and Cats (Stick and Stamp series) by Jason Hook (Quarto Children's Books, 2000)

Starting with Cats by Birgit Golman (Blandford Books, 1997)

Video

Animal Pets Video (Dorling Kindersley)

CD-ROMs

Cats 4 (Mindscape)

Multimedia Guide to Cats (Focus)

Websites

www.bbc.co.uk/education/schools
BBC education online provides lots of information on animals and pets including pet fact files.

www.rspca.org.uk
The official site of the Royal Society for the Prevention of Cruelty to Animals (RSPCA), with lots of useful information on pet care.

www.lurch.net/pets.htm
A site which gives you advice about how to care for your pet. It also includes pages on the care of your cat plus games, stories and crafts.

Useful addresses

You can write to the RSPCA for advice on pet care. Remember to enclose an A4 stamped and self-addressed envelope for a reply.
Enquiries service, RSPCA, Causeway, Horsham, West Sussex, RH12 1HG.
Tel: 01403 264181

Index

B
balancing 27

C
chasing 13, 25
cleaning 15, 20

D
diseases 19

E
exploring 26
eyes 9, 10, 26

F
food 14, 24, 29
fur 10, 15, 21

G
germs 6, 18
grooming 15, 21

H
hunting 13

M
mating 28
milk 6, 8, 14

P
playing 12, 25
pouncing 13

S
safety 17

scent 23
scratching 22
sleeping 5, 7, 8

T
tail 27
teeth 14
toys 13, 25

V
vaccinations 19
vet 19

W
walking 11
washing 20, 29
whiskers 26

Picture acknowledgements
Angela Hampton Family Life Picture Library 14, 17, 20, 21, 22, 23, 24, 25, 26, 28; NHPA 11; HWPL title page, 19; Gettyone Stone 29; Oxford Scientific Films 4 (F.Cicogna/Overseas), 5 (Herbert Schwind/Okapia), 7 (Herbert Schwind/Okapia), 8 (G.I Bernard), 15 (Marianne Wilding); RSPCA Photolibrary 6 (Ken McKay), 9 (Angela Hampton), 10 (Colin Seddon), 12 (Angela Hampton), 13 (Alan Robinson), 16 (Angela Hampton), 18 (Geoff du Feu), 27 (Geoff du Feu).